ONE HUNDRED WAYS TO

Live with a

Horse Addict

◈

ALSO BY TINA BETTISON

One Hundred Ways for a
Horse to Train Its Human

ONE HUNDRED WAYS TO

Live with a

Horse Addict

BY

Tina Bettison

Illustrations by
Anna Gawryś

HODDER &
STOUGHTON

British Library Cataloguing in Publication Data
A record for this book is available from
the British Library

ISBN -10: 0 340 909331
ISBN -13: 9780340909331

Printed and bound in Great Britain by
Bookmarque Ltd, Croydon, Surrey

The paper and board used in this paperback are natural
recyclable products made from wood grown in sustainable
forests. The manufacturing processes conform to the
environmental regulations of the country of origin.

Hodder & Stoughton
A Division of Hodder Headline Ltd
338 Euston Road
London NW1 3BH
www.madaboutbooks.com

This book is dedicated to
Terry Milward, my English teacher at
secondary school, who banned me from
writing about horses for an entire term
because I was becoming addicted. And
to fellow horse addicts the world over;
you know who you are!

Contents

Introduction

Anyone who has ever had a horse, or knows anyone with a horse, will also know that horses are more addictive than alcohol and narcotics, can be just as expensive and there isn't a Betty Ford clinic anywhere that will cure the addiction.

The one saving grace of a horse addict is that the horse does not share your home so while you have to learn to live with the addiction, you don't have to share your space with the object of affection. Lovers of dog and cat addicts aren't so lucky, so be grateful!

A horse will not leave muddy paw prints in the house nor will it jump on your newspaper when you are trying to read it.

Be grateful that the horse is too big to share the bed with you. You certainly won't wake up with a ball of fluff in your face or that claustrophobic feeling where the mog is sleeping on your chest.

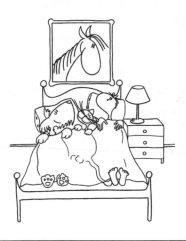

A horse won't scratch the furniture when you go out and leave it on its own, neither will it disturb your neighbours by howling, nor eat its way through your best leather shoes.

A horse won't get into a screeching territorial brawl in the middle of the night right under your window.

A horse won't sit and watch you with a quizzical expression when you are lying in the bath or reading a book on the loo.

A horse has its own house and once you shut the door it stays there until you let it out again. Its litter tray is not as smelly and you don't have to walk it round the block in the rain for it to do its business.

It is most unlikely that your horse addict will nag you to take the horse for a walk.

Horses don't get fleas and take great pride in sharing them with you.

Horses don't have the same penchant as dogs for chewing up important things; nor do they ever strategically vomit up what they have been chewing onto the carpet so you step in it.

A horse won't be occupying your favourite chair when you want to sit in it, and you won't find little swirls of horsehair on the sofa cushions left by the beast itself – only the hairs that have dropped off your addict's jumper.

Well that's the good news … the bad news is …

Although you don't have to live with the horse, you still have to understand the addict. Horse addicts are a little more complicated than their other pet-addict counterparts. For a start there are adult female addicts and pony-mad little girls, which make up the majority of the addict population, and male addicts, which although in a minority have some very specific addict behaviours worth noting. Within these groups there are also different personality types In order to know what you are dealing with before taking an addict on – or to understand the bizarre behaviours of the one you've got, it is worth checking which personality type you might have.

Female Horse Addicts (FHAs)

Female horse addicts come in a plethora of personality types – much more varied than their male equivalents. This is not an exhaustive list!

THE FASHIONISTA

The Fashionista addict is easily spotted. She always has matching, colour-co-ordinated, horse-and-rider wear, in this season's must-have style. When it is out of

fashion, it is out of her wardrobe.
Needless to say her horse never has
a hair out of place either.

THE BARGAIN HUNTER

Her quest is for the best deal and she will spend hours scouring the Internet for the best prices – particularly if the Fashionista is selling last season's stuff on E-bay. Well, it's wise to stock up; you never know when you will need another set of lime-green, leopard- print, polo bandages.

Di Hard-Hunter

(also known as Ms Psycho-Hacker!)

Having had the fear gene removed at birth, this addict comes close to her male compatriot in her need for speed. She will generally be found on a total nutter of a horse, lathered in sweat and breathing fire and brimstone (both horse and rider!).

The Unhappy Hacker

The antithesis of the Di Hard-Hunter, whom she avoids at all costs. The mere thought of galloping in open countryside is enough to send her scuttling back to the tack room to re-clean her pristine tack. Both she and the horse overdose on calming products. She is not good in traffic.

THE DANCING QUEEN

(or Dressage Diva)

Her world is very black and white – i.e. black jackets, white jodhpurs, black boots for her, white boots for the horse. As co-ordinated as the Fashionista, but only in monochrome. She will spend hours polishing and perfecting her moves for a full-on, five-minute performance, and she loves to do it to music.

THE EQUI-BABE

The late-teenage addict who has discovered she can kill two birds with one stone – ride her horse and pull the boys with her perfect be-thonged bottom, tightly clad in breeches.

THE YARD KNOW-IT-ALL

Highly experienced in all horse matters, she will let you share in her knowledge whether you want it or not. Hiding in the stable will not help as she will stand outside the door and share with you anyway. She may also accompany you to the muck heap and back just so you don't miss out on something important that you need to know.

THE SLIGHTLY PSYCHOTIC

Often a very competent rider but with a disturbing tendency to think that everyone else is better than she is. She will worry incessantly about what other people are thinking of her; she will check the competition entries avidly to see whom she is up against. She requires much reassurance and almost as much 'calmer' as the Unhappy Hacker.

The Late Developer

As more women now have their own careers and disposable income, there are an increasing number of addicts who had the childhood fantasies but only fulfilled them in later life. Having re-ignited a latent and dormant passion they may be completely obsessed rather than merely addicted.

MISS CHILLED

Nothing seems to faze her, she wanders through her tasks with a sanguine smile on her face as if in another world. She can be a source of huge irritation to the others when she doesn't participate in their dramas and appears to ignore them. If she ever does lose her rag, it is a firework spectacular which leaves all other types in the shade.

Tell-tale Signs of the FHA

... should you be unsure about the
depth of the addiction

Women collect footwear like a
philatelist collects stamps. The
horse addict's shoe fetish, however, is
less Manolo Blahnik stilettos and
more Sarm Hippique boots. They
cost about the same (i.e. lots of
money) and the principle still applies:
a girl can never have enough ...

The FHA has a wardrobe full of rather nice clothes with the labels still on which she once bought in case she goes somewhere where jodhpurs are not included in the dress code.

She hangs her jodhpurs in the wardrobe in colour order, and owns more of them than any other legwear. She has stretchy ones for 'fat' days and tighter ones for 'slim' days.

A smart jacket means black for affiliated competitions or tweed for riding club. It may also mean the only jacket of any description in the wardrobe not covered in horse slobber.

If you mention top hat and tails she assumes you are a Grand Prix dressage rider rather than best man at a wedding or a contender on *Strictly Come Dancing*.

She can never have enough grooming brushes, stirrup leathers, saddle cloths, lead ropes, fleece rugs and general other paraphernalia. One of each is never enough, and neither is one for each horse.

Her scent is more Cheval No 5 than Chanel. A sweet heady fragrance; top notes of leather balsam and horse slobber, underpinned by a powerful woody base of hay, bedding and droppings, with just a hint of ammonia. This fragrance is occasionally lightened by a floral tone of disinfectant when the stable has its annual thorough clean-out.

The horse addict's home is spotless in the competition season, but only because she actually lives in a horsebox.

If she does venture home, there is usually a trail of straw or shavings behind her so she can find her way back to the yard. Note: avoid dark carpets, particularly red, they really show up the bits! Go for mottled beige.

Mud! The horse addict's car will be plastered with it inside and out, and so will yours if you let her in it. Best to accept it as an integral part of life and your car from October to March and during Wimbledon fortnight.

The FHA has no money. She may start the month with some but by the time she has paid for livery, horse feed, hay, bedding, farrier, back man and other therapies for the horse, supplements, repayments on the 4x4, diesel for the horsebox, competition entries and yet another new saddle-cloth, there won't be any left.

The FHA never has food in her fridge. Assuming she has any money left (see above) she forgets to go shopping and lives on junk and caffeine. Her horse on the other hand has special supplements for all its needs and its feed is agonised over, carefully chosen and measured to ensure optimum nutrition for its workload. Optimum nutrition for you and her is a takeaway.

FHAs generally fall into two categories with regard to make-up and skin care. Either she will be so protective of her skin that she will hoard lotions and potions for every eventuality and wear full make-up to put a barrier between her skin and the elements. Or she has a devil-may-care attitude, does not know what moisturiser is and wears the odd splash of lipstick in a pinkish shade to match her glowing, wind-beaten cheeks.

She usually has a dog (Jack Russells, spaniels and Labradors are favourites), that she can't control but is very cute. If the dog's winter rug matches the horse's, you know you have more than an addict on your hands.

Her bookshelves are heaving with such weighty tomes as *The Equine Body – Cut and Paste Equine Physiology* (yes, it exists, I've got it); *101 Schooling Exercises*; *Another 101 Schooling Exercises*; *Yet More Schooling Exercises* and *Schooling Exercises for Those Who Have Run Out of Ideas Having Read All Other Books on the Subject*.

She will also have the entire series of Thelwell's cartoons and all the books by the Pullein-Thompson sisters. She may even still read them! And every addict over forty will have Pat Smythe's *Jump for Joy*.

Her video collection contains great classics such as *Burghley Horse Trials 1999*, *FEI World Cup 1970*, *Black Beauty*, *Folly Foot* and *Catch your Horse the Easy Way*.

Now You Know She is An Addict . . .

Insist on a separate credit card for horse expenses – that way you will always know exactly where your money is going.

Only ever buy presents that have the word 'horse' somewhere on the label. Fortunately there is such a huge choice of horse-related paraphernalia, you will never be stuck for presents and you never have to worry if she has already got it; as mentioned earlier … a girl can never have enough …!

Get to know your local tack shop and negotiate a frequent-buyer's discount. The 'spend and save' customer loyalty scheme will save you the equivalent of your mortgage per annum.

Have your own interests or you will very rapidly become a groom. Alternatively if you wish to see your beloved addict at all, then give up the golf and pick up a brush.

Becoming jealous and grumpy because your addict seems to spend all her time with the horses is pointless and will only result in her moving in with them. Get involved – poo-picking is a really therapeutic way to unwind after a hard day at the office.

Helping with the mucking-out will ensure you are loved forever. It is wise to get your own pair of rubber gloves though as undoubtedly all the equipment handles will be slightly encrusted. True addicts have no qualms about picking up poo with their bare hands, but that doesn't mean you have to do it too.

If your addict helps out at competitions, you will be roped in. Keep a calculator in your pocket at all times, or brush up on your mental arithmetic, as you are very likely to suddenly find a sheaf of score sheets thrust into your hands for adding up … pronto!

You may be called upon for all manner of little jobs: from picking up a few bales of hay in your company Merc (little bits of which will be stuck like Velcro to the inside of your boot forever) to knocking together a mounting block, *Blue Peter*-style.

You will also be required to brave howling gales and side-on winds to erect electric fencing. The first time you unravel the fencing tape, it's an easy job. Once the tape has been moved around several times, has several short bits tied together and winds itself into knots, it becomes a little more of a challenge.

Note the existence or absence of rosettes when your addict returns from a show before saying anything, especially 'How did it go?' In either case have a G&T at the ready – and an extra large one for you.

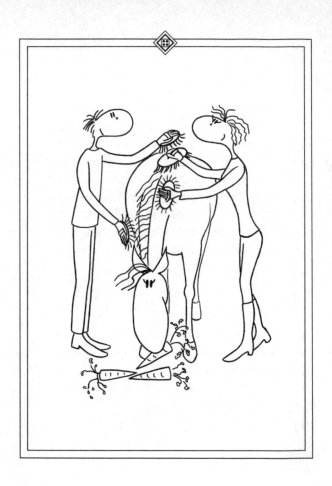

Teamwork with your addict is a wonderful thing; it rarely happens, but just on occasion the harmony of two people working together is like dancing without blackened toes. One of you de-rugs, the other rugs up; one prepares feeds, the other fills water buckets; one moans a lot, the other lets it go in one ear and out the other.

To avoid unnecessary disappoint-
ment, remember the existence of
highly polished boots and a couple of
schooling whips in the bedroom does
not mean your luck is in and a wild
night is on the cards.

Be prepared to forgo holidays or get
used to going on your own. Always
assuming that your loved one will actually
leave the horse for longer than a few
hours, and has the back-up of a livery
yard or good friend who can look after
the beastie, you will have to put up with
constant phone calls to check beastie is
OK and not missing her too much.

The odd weekend break may be possible, but three weeks' long haul is most unlikely, even if it's your honeymoon. Just accept the horse comes first; it will save much heartache later.

Horses are herd animals and it is every addict's dream to have her own herd. Some crave the patter of tiny feet and are just not fulfilled unless they have produced their own little one. In which case there will be great agonising over the right father – hair colour, bone structure, intelligence, temperament. Choosing an appropriate stallion is akin to vetting boyfriends, except that it doesn't matter how many sexual partners the stallion has had; a herd of offspring is actually a prerequisite.

Growing the herd by acquisition rather than reproduction may be the preferred method of your addict. Be aware that unless you are also an addict you have no say in this matter. You may have an opinion, but only if it agrees with hers.

If your addict is of the charitable nature, horse sales are best avoided. She won't be able to choose just one and will probably try to save them all, for fear that they will end up with the meat man. On the upside, keeping a 100-head herd in the garden will ensure you have prize roses in the village flower show.

Even the strongest of addicts may succumb to a dubious acquisition if the horse in question is about to be written off. Beware of phone calls from your addict's friends on a mercy mission. Exactly how many companion horses does she need?

Acquisition of a performance horse is a different matter. You will be grilled for your opinion, though it may be ignored. And when the final decision is made and the vetting passed, you will get out your chequebook and (smiling) pay for it because she has of course spent all her money on keeping the other horses she has already acquired.

The Pony-mad Child (PMC)

(boys do not always follow
the same pattern)

Addiction starts at an early age. Every little girl seems to become obsessed with ponies somewhere around the age of six to eight years old. Some then become obsessed with boys but the sensible ones stick with the pony addiction.

Every waking hour is consumed by thoughts of ponies. Every night time ponies fill her dreams. Her imagination is inspired by her fantasy horses; coats gleaming as the sunlight bounces off their flanks. An entire parallel existence occupies the mind of the pony-mad girl – and she occupies this place more often than not, particularly when it is homework time.

Beware of damping creative enthusiasm. There is only one subject worthy of writing or drawing, or covering your wall if you are a PMC, and that is ponies, ponies, ponies!

For little girls, their world of ponies is a mix of magic and myth, a fantasy where anything is possible. From grooming and preening to sharing wild adventures, their pony is their best friend and their confidante – whether it is real or imaginary.

In the absence of a real pony, the PMC will prance about as if she is one. She will trot instead of run, canter instead of skip and frequently put in the odd neigh, snort or a spot of head-shaking. Don't be alarmed, this is normal behaviour and she will grow out of it – usually around fifty-ish.

If it has a pony on it, whatever it is, or even mentions the word, it will be desired, coveted, pocket money saved for and the subject of much pleading. Actually that is still the case whatever the age of the addict, it's just that the older she gets the bigger the toys become.

Every Christmas there will be the must-have pony toy, which you absolutely have to get if you want to avoid the devastation of a disappointed daughter; even if you have to ship it in from some far-flung place at a vastly inflated price.

The PMC also used to spend the entire weekend at the local riding stables helping out in return for a free ride. Whether plaiting *all* the ponies tails was absolutely necessary is a matter of opinion.

Remember the Britains' riding stable? Two hundred plastic horses all with strange posts sticking out of their backs would roam across the living-room carpet, causing much anguish to anyone who stepped on one.

When you are the parent of a pony-obsessed child, you are dragged into it whether you like it or not. You might be washing real tails or brushing the tangle out of toy ones. You have to read the same books, and many a parent has been spotted hiding their novel inside a copy of the latest pony story.

It is wonderful when the whole family can get involved. It starts with the local gymkhana and for the odd ambitious few ends up at the Olympics. You catch the addiction of seeing your little angel carrying off the red rosettes and suddenly every weekend you are embroiled in grooming, preening, shining and polishing. Beware of sibling rivalry, hell hath no fury like the child who came second.

Also beware of falling to the trap of 'keeping up with the Joneses'. No matter what your child's friends have, you do not need a splendid, state-of-the-art horsebox that travels six, when you have one 12.2 pony; a trailer will do.

Pony-mad boys do exist too, but they are unlikely to be found in a bedroom covered with pony posters, pony bedcovers, and every pony accessory available covering every surface. Like their adult male counterparts they like the rough and tumble, they will be cowboys and

Indians, brave battle-weary soldiers or
Grand National jockeys; they and
their ponies soaked in sweat from
galloping about, saving the world.

Long-suffering fathers of PMCs past were cajoled into building an entire set of show jumps for the lawn, which were leapt over at great speed by PMC and her little addict chums as they pretended to be Geoff Glazzard, Harvey Smith, David Broome and Graham Fletcher. Many of today's young addicts pretend to be Pippa Funnell on a CD Rom.

Male Horse Addicts (MHAs)

A different breed altogether

Some male addicts are born with the horse-addiction gene, others have it thrust upon them. I have found they fall into three general categories:

Category 1 Male Addict

Horses are a means of escapism. He has a horse instead of a garden shed. He potters about the yard instead of the garden, and will spend hours grooming his charge instead of weeding and growing

things. His horse is not a machine, it is a sentient being, and he may love it more than his spouse. He is the closest a male can get to being a female addict.

Cat. 1 male does not, however, have any of the purchasing habits of the female of the species. In this he is very much akin to his Cat. 2 and 3 male compatriots. However, unlike them the word 'competition' does not enter his vocabulary. The most he does with his beastie is a gentle wander round the lanes listening to the birds.

CATEGORY 2 MALE ADDICT

This guy's life revolves around his horse. But he has a completely different relationship with his horses from the female addict or from the Cat. 1 male. It is the activities he is

addicted to rather than the horse itself (or so he says), and God forbid he should admit to having a soft spot for his beast (though he does really).

Whereas the female addict will return home frequently (to check she still has one), you won't see the Cat. 2 male from the beginning of his season until the end. He assumes someone is home holding the fort and feeding the children.

He is most likely to be found doing something fast, furious, dangerous and sweaty, though some of the more sensitive types do enjoy dressage for its skill and grace. His horse is his trusty companion and accomplice in his adventures. He still believes he is the Lone Ranger.

CATEGORY 3 MALE ADDICT

An acquired addiction is often the worse kind. A Cat. 3 male may start out as the groupie to his female addict, but before long he has taken over and is running the competitive show. Overnight he becomes an authority on everything equine and his opinion is king.

The Cat. 2 or 3 male is addicted to competition. Observers may look upon a polo chukka, a steeplechase, a cross-country event or a driving trial as mere sport, but it is in fact an ancient battlefield of testosterone, a test of male dominance and prowess, where winning is paramount in the survival of the fittest and best.

The female of the addictive species has horses to build a relationship with. The Cat. 3 male probably has a more intimate relationship with the horsebox than the horse. He makes sure the horsebox works. She follows his instructions to ensure the horse works. This he calls teamwork.

Behavioural Differences Between FHAs and MHAs

MHA has no truck with this namby-pamby colour co-ordinated rubbish. If it is really lucky, his horse might get a rug. Any old rug will do and as long as one of the straps does up it is just fine.

The MHA will have one grooming brush and use it only when absolutely necessary, such as at a competition. Though he is unlikely to wield it himself. He'll get one of his groupies to do it for him, and toss them a lascivious smile as a reward.

The FHA may feel torn between her horses and her home, and be wracked with guilt whichever one she chooses. No male addict has the word 'guilt' in his vocabulary.

FHAs are frequently concerned about what others think of them, particularly at a competition. For the MHA only one opinion matters and that is his own. If the judge doesn't agree then he/she is clearly blind.

Interestingly the male addict uses the same fragrance as the female – Cheval No 5; but without the disinfectant.

Whereas the FHA calls home frequently when away to check if her horse is missing her, the MHA calls home frequently to check if the person caring for his horse is following his instructions.

The MHA believes he is in full control of his horse at all times, which gives him a sense of power and purpose. His horse just lets him believe this for a quiet life – as do the females in his world.

The MHA has one pair of boots (two if he is a professional rider) and cannot fathom why anyone would need more than that. He absolutely cannot understand why a female addict has so many – she can only ride in one pair at once, can't she?

The MHA has a fridge only to keep his beer in. Left totally to his own devices, he is in fact worse than the female at consuming a nutritionally balanced diet and can live on curry for weeks. He isn't always pleasant to live with.

While the female addict can and will collect anything that says 'horse' on it in triplicate, the male collects practical things one at a time and only replaces them when they are totally useless. Hence he will still be using virtually hairless brushes, frayed lead ropes and tack held together with string where the female will see any excuse for more retail therapy.

If you are dating an elusive MHA then be aware that 'I am playing polo this weekend' is probably a euphemism for something entirely different, particularly if he vaguely mentions a change of mount for every chukka.

If there are shining boots and schooling whips in the bedroom, your luck is definitely in and a wild night most probably is on the cards.

An MHA combined with DIY addict is definitely a double-edged sword. On the one hand all those little jobs like sticky stable doors could no longer be the bane of your life; on the other ... all those started-but-unfinished DIY jobs could be multiplied many-fold.

If something goes wrong, the female addict will always look to herself first and ask, 'What did I do?'; the male addict will look at the horse and say, ' You stupid ********.'

Horse Addicts Anonymous

No such organisation exists, but we could always start one if partners of addicts become really desperate. As the old saying goes: you can lead a horse to water but you can't make it drink. Same applies to addicts!

Addicts have been known to migrate their addiction, just as drug addicts may kick the drugs but then become alcoholics. Horse addicts may give up team-chasing, but then get hooked on carriage-driving instead; or give up jumping and become dressage queens.

They have been known to change allegiances between breeds too. The love of a nippy little thoroughbred ex-race horse with a great jump may become an unquenchable desire for a big-boned warm blood with an extension to die for. Torn between an

expressive Andalusian or a fun and
funky Icelandic, the addict may buy
both but hide one in a friend's yard
away from the prying eyes of the
partner.

ONE CAN IMAGINE A HAA MEETING:

Wild-eyed woman admits to stealing money from her partner's wallet to feed her habit: 'I had to, the farrier was standing there, expecting his dues. I'd spent it all at the feed merchants. I had to get it from somewhere! I'll pay it back!'

Second wild-eyed woman, weeping inconsolably: ' My husband! How could he do that to me? After all the years we have been together!' The group leans forward in support.

Has he left her? Run off with a non-addict? But no. 'He beat me at the Nationals! That trophy was mine and he knew it!'

Deeply worried man: 'I couldn't resist her. I knew it was wrong, but I couldn't help myself. She kept fluttering her eyelashes and begging me to ride her. She wanted it! We galloped over the fields, leapt hedges – the adrenaline, the buzz. I know I'd do it again. But the risk … if my girlfriend ever finds out … her best dressage horse …'

Woman with her priorities straight: 'He has 200 acres, twenty stables, a 60x20 ménage and an Oakley Supreme 6. Of course I love him!'

Woman with a real shopping habit: 'I tried to keep it a secret. I hoped no one would notice an extra one. OK, so he was the only dark bay in the field. So what's one more?!

Male with secret horse obsession: 'I thought I'd been so careful. I had hidden my copy of *Horse and Hound* under the mattress and I only ever read it tucked into *Play Boy* so she wouldn't suspect anything. Apparently I'm just a sucker for a pretty filly ... but she did have nice fetlocks.'

Once an addict; always an addict! You certainly can't beat 'em, so save the heartache and join 'em!